I S I T A T I O N

VISITATION

Maggie Blake Bailey

**TINDERBOX
EDITIONS**

ISBN: 978-1-943981-15-1

Tinderbox Editions
Molly Sutton Kiefer, Publisher and Editor
Red Wing, Minnesota
tinderboxeditions@gmail.com
www.tinderboxeditions.org

Cover design by Nikkita Cohoon
Cover artwork, "Solstice II" by Hélène Delmaire
Interior design by Nikkita Cohoon
Author photo by Mary Stafford Zirkle

For my daughter and son

Contents

Carolina Wrens 5

There Will Be No Thunderstorms Tomorrow 6

Driving Past Midnight Through Rural Tennessee 8

When I Became a Mother 9

Portrait in Wikipedia Entry for Subutex 10

Buzzards Bay 11

Mary Listens 12

Reservoir 13

Ownership 14

Rosemary Called Minnow 15

Showing My Daughter a Pelican 16

Post-Partum OCD 17

Horses 18

Town Politely Waits for Dead Whale to Explode 19

Bridges Freeze Before Roads 22

Egret 23

Honeysuckle 24

Mary Remembers 26

Moths 27

Break My Hands 28

Annunciation 29

Clam Digging 30

Red Right Returning 31

Bless 32

Mary admits, ... 33

Fiddler Crab 34

Oophorectomy* 35

A Body Made of Bees 36

Wedding Gift for a Man I Once Imagined Marrying 37

Non-native 38

Before the First Snow 39

Glacier Climbing.. 40
An Answer to the Popular Google Search: How Do
Hummingbirds Sleep?... 42
Portrait in Wikipedia Entry for Ativan 43
Mary had a mother named 44
Larches... 45
Fever Before Delivering 46
Nativity 48
The Body, After 49
Holy Mary, Mother of the Epidural 50
Offering 51
Postpartum... 52
Elizabeth Wants... 53
The Fisherman's Wife 54
For Jen, the Day After Your Stroke 55
Dusk, St Simon's Island... 56
Flathead Lake 57
A Love Poem for Ellen, Ten Years Late.......................... 58
November 59
Plate Tectonics 60
The Last Dog.. 61
Carrion Birds 62
Portrait in Wikipedia Entry for Fentanyl 63
At Twenty-Six Weeks, A Fetus Starts Dreaming............. 65
Parking Lot 67
To Stone... 68
Elizabeth Asks 69

VISITATION

Visitation, *n.*

The action of going to a place, either for some special purpose or merely in order to see it.

The action, on the part of animals, of resorting to a particular place at certain seasons, or of exceptionally appearing in places which are not their usual habitat.

The action, on the part of God or some supernatural power, of coming to, or exercising power over, a person or people for some end:

> In order to encourage, comfort, or aid.
> In order to test, try, examine, or judge.

The visit paid by the Virgin Mary to Elizabeth, recorded in Luke i. 39.

—OED

Carolina Wrens

for Rick Barot

The definition of metaphor
is *the transfer of burden,*
so pay attention.

There is the heron of my longing:
the curve of neck, stilt of legs,
blue, breakable, prone to flight.

The summer of my certainty:
lit with streaks of a fox's tail
slipping back into the woods.

The house of my mother's madness:
worn front steps lost
to waist-high weeds and debt.

Now watch a small bird building
her nest inside a watering can,
darting each piece of straw through

the one round opening.
Imagine a chick learning
to fly by launching itself skyward,

the stunned drop to the can's bottom,
rattle of wings inside metal,
mocking blue coin of sky,
and name it.

There Will Be No Thunderstorms Tomorrow

*For the first time since early in the morning on
February 11, no thunderstorms are predicted anywhere in
the United States*

—The Vane *10/16/14*

Instead we will turn to each other, only now
realizing who sits at our table,

and say, *I didn't know,* because we cannot say,
Did you see that storm today?

Because we cannot touch each other, even lightly,
in passing. There is no release without payment,
and payment is measured in damage.

I will not hear you talk in your sleep
and you will not brace your sodden body to mine.

No power will go out, no dogs will shake in the corners
as we light candle stubs with long matches.

Instead I will wake late, convinced
it is a different tomorrow, one threaded with salt
and metal brought in over the Atlantic,

I will open our windows to a sky that is blue and blue
and purple, the color of the child inside
of me, breathing water.

I will name my body fore and aft and rolling.
There will be no fog warnings, buoys stuttering
like mouths without tongues, dumb in the sunshine.

For the first time we are radar with nothing to see.

Driving Past Midnight Through Rural Tennessee

My headlights seek the lawn jewelry
of campaign signs, the sleeping,
obscene zucchini left unpicked,

the one white cow that could have flicked
my high beams back to me, tucked away
and sleeping in a low barn.

Past the low fur of road kill,
the cornfields that break for churches,
each church a brick leaning against the night,

I count the flash of highway
markers strobing the miles beside me,
while my daughter,

a sightless stowaway, touches only
the landmarks of her own hands,
our bodies in transit and not yet home.

When I Became a Mother

My own mother said: If you keep chewing
on your hair it will ball up in your heart
and kill you. Said: I dreamt I picked the flesh
off her bones like a chicken wing. Left it scattered
on your father's windshield. Said: I bargained for your
heartbeat. But bargains are just nesting dolls. One
opening, coming loose in your hands, spilling out
another: click after click after click.

Portrait in Wikipedia Entry for Subutex

The treatment phase   veered away
continual use   behaves differently

can essentially be thought of as   human studies
requires both

the presence of light   the desirable actions

Buzzards Bay

Sometimes lightning is just a pulse,
not a jagged line of mythic anger—
everything yellow then not.

My new daughter sleeps better in the binding
weight of thunder and the tight hold of
rain. One arm flung out across the world
of her crib, she learns each evening how to
prolong her submersion, her wordless night.

In all my summers on Buzzards Bay
I have never seen a buzzard, only the sharp
glint of an osprey wheeling toward her nest,
tracing the swells of air and bringing feathers
and talons to rest, like a finial, like a saint.

Sky and water lit in tandem, the osprey feeds
her daughter pieces of light, while mine
sighs and murmurs beside an open
window. Her first summer, soaked to the bone.

Mary Listens

Then Mary said to the angel, "How can this be, since I do not know a man?"

—*Luke 1:34*

Elizabeth says: *here.*
Turn your body.
Hold the water pitcher

and empty what can be emptied.
These saviors are here to stay.

But the flat bread
chewed slowly at dawn,
is it a relic now?

Someday they will hoard
his toenails, lavish gold
on his finger bones.

But I cannot imagine they will
pray the litany of meconium,
the rosary of linea nigra.

We were never meant to have blood.
I never said my body
was a cathedral.

Elizabeth says: *here. Open*
your hand against the light.

Reservoir

We lower our July bodies
to immersion, some shell
of the world breaking open
to water.   Legs cut through
to colder layers, pale skin
flashes the language of must,
will, and watch me.

Ownership

I used to make beets slip
off their skin under cold water,
say sugar, when they wanted
to say dirt. I owned every hornet
that nested humming, restless,
underneath my threshold.

I spoke cranes to the edge
of a quiet lake, folded their wings
shut against the swoop
of their bodies, fed them fish
slick and silver from my lungs.
Now I use my days to count
your breaths, I still my hands
and lighten my sleep, I mortgage
myself for the rise of your chest.

Rosemary Called Minnow

My mother's second child
was her first loss.

A daughter nicknamed Minnow,
the sharp silver baitfish of tidal change.

Fluid filled her skull, so they toured
institutions: saw her future in permanent

infants, their heavy heads bent under
liquid. It didn't matter. Minnow never

left the hospital. The child waiting at home,
my brother, lived settled against the weight

of loss, a sibling's wish granted: *Lord,*
I don't want a sister.

Showing My Daughter a Pelican

Horizon birds, my grandfather would say,
*look, they have fish in the soft scoop
of their mouths, their throats.*

The pelican stands at the end
of a summer town pier, past the crabbers,
the sticky hands of children

eating ice cream, all the white flesh
burnt pink at the elastic waist bands,
old tank tops, the fat at the back of the neck.

I am surprised by ugliness:
the open circle of weathered dock,
no one wanting to get close to the bird

that seems more dinosaur more monster,
a bird painted into Bibles because scholars
believed it killed its young, and then,

contrite, resurrected them with drops
of blood from its own breast,
Christ-like. But that isn't true.

What would I have said to my daughter
even if they did? Better to invent
our own mythology.

She was there, she saw the pelican.
She has started life knowing wings,
throats, and nothing of contrition.

Post-Partum OCD

Walking down the stairs I hear
my daughter say: *One, two,*
though it sounds like *won, shoe.*

She repeats it all the way down:
Won, shoe, won, shoe.

She hears me, in my panic,
counting each stair I walk down
when I hold her hand.

The doctor named it.

But I know I need to be vigilant:
against stairs and water and scissors.
Cars and drivers and pavement.

I didn't mean for her to mimic me.

I won't stop counting.

Horses

for Ryan Sample

I say, *tell me about horses,*
Montana horses…

And you say,
I saw one fall down a gully
off a cliff-side trail once.

And I imagine a clattering of limbs,
the burning shriek of a horse

suddenly sideways,
hooves sparking against granite.

That teeth and eyes and
clouds are the same relentless white,

that without obstacle, freefall
hardens ligaments into wire.

Instead you say:
We went back the next day and watched
grizzlies feast on the poor thing.

Town Politely Waits for Dead Whale to Explode

I

It's strange what can force a town to wait.
The awkward insistence of a dead whale,
the late-night arguments at Patterson's,
old men suggesting dynamite, chainsaws,
funneling gasoline down the blow hole,

and just letting the damn thing burn for days.
All we talk about now is how to erase
what we can't move, can't kill and can't bury.
The priest each Sunday finds new images:
we wait for God like we wait for a whale

to finally explode, or we're the whale
that God is waiting for, but we wonder
how faith could possibly smell like this.
We stop mowing our lawns, tending our rows
of vegetables. What is the point, we ask,

waiting for the sky to rain blubber and guts.
The weeds make the most of our small rebellion.
Our sons think only of water balloons.
Red rubber turning pink against
the strain of tap water, how hard it was

to tie the knot, the burst against a back,
a leg, or shoes. While our golden retrievers
twitch, dreaming of smells that say: *survive
and you will never go hungry again*

II

Relief smells like an ocean left to rot.
Relief hurts like blood or a heartbeat.

III

The wet kiss of whale meat ruins the clean
white shirts of a Monday morning, wraps veins
like bracelets on arms that meant only to hold
open a door, rolls the hula hoop
slice of an artery past teenagers waiting

for the bus, car alarms announce the slap
of dorsal fins on windshields, and hoods,
as saltwater sluices through gutters,
pushes half-eaten krill into the half-
hearted creeks that flank the interstate.

IV

Sweeping the fat off the roads takes weeks,
and schools cancel class in the face of rot,
history and math driven out by the stench
of grease and muscle caught in heating ducts
folds of skin snagged in the slats of benches,
baleen tangled in swings and bicycle spokes.

These days we travel with bleach and tweezers,
wash our sheets again and again each night,
our dinner tables are silent and thick
with the rancid scent of aftermath
under our nails, in our hair, on our tongues.
We have nothing to say to each other now.

V

The rotten heart, still as big as a car,
settles into sand by the boardwalk like
a piece of modern art, and we talk now,
not of chainsaws, anger, and gasoline,
but of pocket knives, stealth, and Tupperware.
We were patient, and we want our relief to last.

Bridges Freeze Before Roads

and roads freeze before rivers,
fish fall asleep before birds,
and birds sink before helium,
which freezes last, in a math
known as freezing point
depression, but I'm not sure
how math will save us when

one fawn lies down to sleep
and in the morning, ice holds
hooves, black nose, and thin,
sick haunches to the ground,
marrow red because the body
ate the fat that keeps it white.

Or when a person freezes, sheds
his clothes in an act known as
paradoxical undressing,
one last chance to see cold
as a blessing or an answer.

So when you are hungry
for causation, blame the bridges
for the first tendrils of ice that
kicked the whole world into winter,
always blame the first to go.

Egret

I am holding my daughter when the egret
flashes into view, catching me between wonders.
If I reach for paper, my daughter will stir.
The crook of my arm braces her still heavy head
and the weight of my hands steadies hers.

I used to record the detailed truth of each egret
as it walked past. Now in motherhood, writing
is memory, a bird conjured days later, the stiff edge
of feathers imprecise. Egret as reference.
Time measured in how many egrets ago.

Even the memory of egrets will run dry, so I imagine
one instead, an impossible egret. It pushes its sharp
face to the glass, opens both wings in the light.
Veins like rivers divide the translucent body.
My daughter slips deeper asleep, still small enough

to be calmed by the tide of my pulse. All
wonder and white feathers desert me. I hold her while
I can. She murmurs and sighs. She dreams a visitation
of cardinals, braiding through trees, burning red and joyful.

Honeysuckle

is taste not scent,
memory pulling
a blossom apart:

we craved
the green edge of it,
scouted branches

in June, walked
barefoot, our clothes
sour with seawater.

We pissed in the ocean,
let our burns peel,
as we searched our

bodies for ticks,
fat with blood,
seaweed

tangled in creases,
as we pried off
bathing suits under

rust-tinged showers
of well water.
We counted spider

bites, ran our hands
over the soft fat

of thighs, and built
constellations of ache.

Mary Remembers

Now indeed, Elizabeth your relative has also conceived a son in her old age; and this is now the sixth month for her who was called barren.

—*Luke 1:36*

Elizabeth had myrrh.
After the last lost baby,
Zacharias bought her a small jar.

At night, she worked the salve
into her cracked hands
that folded and refolded the linen

of their bed, unblessed until angels
came to say otherwise.
And I came to her door.

For a spell, we anchored together,
rounded bellies turning in the dark,
reciting our stations of ache and hope.

Elizabeth would place her thumbs
where my neck met my shoulders
when no one else touched me.

Tonight these men give
back to me the scent of that room.

Everyone else gets to have birds.
I want her hands to push me apart.

Moths

My son sleeps, so I sleep

and dream that right below my knee,
my skin puckers into peaks.

When I press, the heads of moths
push through,
and in one motion, I pluck the bright
insects from my body.

Even though I draw them out
as fast as I can,
color sings at the edge
of my vision.

I can see the wings:
jeweled red and blue,
folded and slick against
the long moth bodies;
my legs alive and empty.

Break My Hands

Tallahassee, Atlanta, Columbia.
Sarah is reciting state capitals.

When she was six years old,
she asked her father to break her hands.

I think about hands cracked
between a hammer and a wooden

table, slammed in a door frame or held
too hard, too long. Sarah and I, we want

one startling, brilliant pain.
I join her incantation, building slight relief

as we venture west, clicking each name into place:
Sacramento, Olympia, Salem.

Sarah finds the transplanted freckles of Hawaii,
the excised mass of Alaska floating in a blue,

waveless Pacific, water hemmed
against islands splayed out like broken

joints. Her hand comes to rest in the lower
left corner and together we say Juneau,

knowing the effort facts demand,
tasting conviction like honey. Thick
tongued, we settle for the lesser satisfaction.

Annunciation

Hold up two fingers and command me
to build the tabernacle my heart
could not bear itself.

Your arm hooked between the blades
of my back has become a fettering
and breaking wing.

Bound to take flight, bound by you,
by how well you fit and fill.
Hold me still.

Clam Digging

For my father

Salt skin and the tin smell of the sea dying.
To the mouth of the tide, I take
myself and a yellow plastic bucket.

Where the shore turns black, I scan for holes,
bubbles, breathing in the ground,
and then I dig, submerged fingers blind.

The shell feels a curve of a calcium house.
Through the suction of the water, I work
down its ridges, grasp it before I take it

and hold open the path of departure. Forget this
and my thumb is lost inside the slick
belly of a young one broken through.

At night we steam the rest open, pry
the flesh loose and drag it in butter
so all we taste is fat and the sea.

Red Right Returning

We replace Georgia's blistering
June with the double named edge
of New England:
horse flies, sand fleas, deer ticks.
A plague to be outside.

In the heat, we verge on thunder
storms, we stack sunrises
on buoys, we say *red right returning*,
as a way through rough water
because everything is bloom and thorn:

Queen Anne's lace and beach
plum, one osprey waiting to dive,
frenzied minnows, blackberries
still red and hard in the hand,
fog moving in against the weir.

Bless

As you walk through July, bless the burn of your thighs,
the holy heat of the creases beneath your breasts
that hold lint and pooling sweat.

You command the sway of a back that meets waist
in ridges and folds. Yours is the heft and dig
of bras built with technical precision.

Not for you the limp lace of a halter or balconette.
Instead, bless these fistfuls of belly until you can rest,
in your body, our body, mine.

Mary admits,

I never have another child.
They need me when his body
seeks mine, small mouth turning
to breast. But I am still hungry.

And Your promise is
a broken body and the spectacle
of limbs in my arms, cradled
like a newborn. Your miracle
is for the men at the cave.

My body is an advent calendar,
so offer me:

a baby that latches, small face slack,
lips painted in milk. A way to put
my body back together in a winter
made of undemanding darkness.

Fiddler Crab

Cousin of the Ghost Crab,
I slide at night into pale,
my shell fades and surges,
its own perfect camouflage.
Come morning, I use my mouth
to shift mud, sift sludge,
and feed on waste and algae.
I am both gilled and lunged,
the tide-line a threshold I cross
sideways, pulled by unevenness.
What I lose, I remake:
this hand, impossible to
remove. I have wrenched it
off only to find what remains
bloating, swelling, rising
to keep me playing, a new
smaller mate blossoming
at the ragged site of removal.
What would you give,
to always be, no matter
the damage, the same?

Oophorectomy*

A long drift upward through
opium and night sweats,
glue and blood patched across
a body knitting against itself.

When I turn in my sleep, nothing
brakes the body's momentum,
nothing says the gravity inside me
has been rearranged.

I am secretly uneven, a future
motherhood cut in half, two
faint lines etched above
my hip bones.

For days I walk slowly, one hand
braced against the revolt
of another organ, the collusion of
a greater defiance within me.

* *surgical removal of one or both ovaries*

A Body Made of Bees

Hard to be Mary,
heart set on a visit
to the only other woman
with swollen ankles.

A chance to say:
No one ever touched me.

An afternoon spent
almost asleep—
in sunlight like honey,
in a body made of bees.

The word they give her
is *mediatrix*.

As if I would pray
to the tallest tree
and not the lightning.

As if her body hadn't
done all the work:
immaculate construction
of hive.

Oh to be golden, thick
and slow with heaven.

Wedding Gift for a Man I Once Imagined Marrying

Enough crows to fill the drawers
of your dresser.

Tan horses with black tails,
their nervous laughter running practice
scales up and down the coming darkness.

Heat lightning and wildfire smoke
in a flask for your breast pocket.

Mountains that forget themselves and tip
backwards into mornings
the same bruised yellow as
Scotch burning the back of your mouth.

That you find tomorrow
as staggering and wholly unneeded
as a handful of teeth.

Non-native

*"People said, 'You can't raise elk in Florida.' But we are, so
I guess you can," says Up River manager James Brown Jr.*

In the Smoky Mountains, elk,
made of roadside ice and hoarfrost,
come out of the fog
and settle back in, like river
rocks, with antlers meant to rise
from creeks and branches,
startling thrush and wren.

Where we have taken them,
the air bristles with sand.
One elk finds the shoreline
of Lake Okeechobee,
remembers winter, pauses,
and waits to catch
the bronze glint of turkey feathers,
white pulse of a doe.

It dips a furred mouth hoping
to taste snowmelt, oak.
Instead, hooves strike against
limestone as small bream ribbon past.
The elk kneels, smudging
eelgrass and peppergrass
with long suffering limbs,
closes eyes still rimmed
in midges, and dreams back.

Before the First Snow

comes, the first frost rims
the bay in white, salts
the field, shows the tidal
river course like a vein
on the inside of a wrist.

The wind smells of sap, metal,
groans against the settling house.
The snow that follows drives
slanted, pressing east, collecting
against one wall of each barn,

one face of each jetty, lining
the branches of stunted pines,
doubling the limbs that stretch
into late sky, a second version
stamped in snow. One side waits,

clean and brown, every break
of bark apparent. The other offers
blank submission to winter.
Two versions of the same fury
that sound-proofed the air.

Walking home, looking left,
each pine shows a clean face.
A wooded, living falsehood:
it never snowed, it is only
evening, come a little soon.

Glacier Climbing

The first time in the emergency room,
she said it was grapefruit juice,
a bad reaction.

I didn't know what Fentanyl was,
that they found patches all over her body,
I thought addiction announced itself:

a fire or an earthquake, but instead
my mother can't keep her eyes open,
forgets my daughter's name.

Like a cathedral pressing against
its own arches, she tries to steady
the teeth in her mouth.

II

Years ago, I left to climb a glacier
in Alaska and learned how to cling
to the mountain, how to bracket

my limbs against gravity, carelessness,
learned to yell *FALLING*
when falling.

The biggest threat was dry ice:
a pitted dirty landscape,
rock and fog at the glacier's tail end.

Here is no purchase;
if you stay clipped in and fall,
you just take others with you.

I thought I would know when I lost
my mother, that her weight,
for so long tied to mine,

would pull me down into grief.
Instead, the fog has set in,
and I can't see my hands.

An Answer to the Popular Google Search: How Do Hummingbirds Sleep?

When hummingbirds sleep,
they go into a hibernation-like state,
their body temperature will drop
to the point of becoming hypothermic.

Who cares what we are
if we know how to slow our blood.
Then winter becomes nighttime
and all this loss is dreaming.

Portrait in Wikipedia Entry for Ativan

unpleasant awake
             behavioral disinhibition

both explicit and implicit memory
             dose-dependent

such stress and frustration in the first place
             unsteady

the patient's ability to protect
             reduced

validity challenged
             must use chaperones

        the ease of addiction.   potentially embarrassing or criminal

This explains why
             half-lives

an acceptable trade-off
             eventually

the brain has
             voltage

Mary had a mother named

Anne, the apocryphal mother, written in margins,
written in saints' books. She was barren, too—
it seems angels prefer the desperate.

Anne, old and empty, willing to make a deal.
Willing to promise a daughter away
to the convent if the angel just lets her

bear the child: an immaculate conception
and forgotten mother, all so that Mary could show up
in the story unencumbered.

Anne always ready to tell her daughter—
Believe the angels. Offer them anything.
You won't get to keep the child anyway.

What if Mary had been able to say—
Mother, what should I do?
And Anne was alive to say, *Lie. Go home, seduce*
him tonight, and say the child came early.

But Mary's mother was already dead,
and really, how much is a mother worth
when we are working toward the Father and the Son.

Larches

Larches drop needles
all year long, their brown branches
tilting away from the sun.
When my mother visits, I hear
her through the walls, crying
in her sleep. How many years
this exact sound, frequency. Tonight
is the smallest full moon of the year,
so I shut all the doors against
her pain— watch the sharp light,
zinc and anemic, pin the sky.

Fever Before Delivering

In January, a fever has two hands
to grip and wring you clean.
The sweat you wake up in,
wet and sticking under your breasts,
at the nape of your neck,
makes you remember the way
your mother once braided your hair,
a pigtail down each shoulder,
so you could wake from an illness
with no tangles from your thrashing.

The sweat is for your own good,
you will be cleaner for it,
but you can't cheat the healing,
which will take days without seams.

When you wake, you will be scoured
like a pan with steel wool, you will be
the right kind of mother. Before you
step into the hot clarity of your better
self, run your tongue down the salt lick
of that hallucination-wrecked sleep,
taste your fear that you don't want her,
that she will cry and you will walk
out of the room, out of the house, and leave
your small daughter pulsing in the dark.

Taste your desire to write her,
instead of hold her. Choose words acidic
and clean, like rosewater, like the frozen

ocean you saw in your sleep last night.
In January, a fever has two hands
to grip and wring you clean. Let it.

Nativity

Myrrh smells like licorice.
Frankincense smells like lemon
and pine sap.

Birth smells like blood and shit.
The body loses half itself.
How much straw is stained?

When the men anoint the boy,
who gathers the limbs
of the mother?

Who gathers the gold?

The Body, After

I expected the spreading lowlands
of my thighs, I expected fat breasts,
hardening to the rhythm of my daughter's
hunger, the purple creases that mark
like a wound, as if a jellyfish had wrapped
herself around me, filaments of burn.
I don't believe in my body now,
hanging loose, draped across bones
like canvas drenched in rain.
My body tangles and seeps, buckles
over itself. My body rests and pools.
My softness says: *you were full.*
You are full beyond capacity.

Holy Mary, Mother of the Epidural

Much to the wisemen's dismay,
Mary continues to bleed for weeks.

Mary struggles with low supply,
buys teas and vitamins on the internet.

Mary considers co-sleeping in hay,
decides to sleep-train

but no one lets him cry.

The Mary I knelt to
dressed in white and robin's egg blue.

I am a mother now and
my son sleeps in my arms.

His rest feels hard won
and frightening.

This Mary asks to have her tubes tied.
Fool me once.

Offering

for Anders Carlson-Wee

Driving home, both children crying,
I saw a young deer in the median, pressed
into the dip of grass.
She looked asleep but for the hollowed-out
space below her still furred ribcage.

I don't leave the house much. I'm not even
sure I have a body. Except when I run
my hand over the still angry scar raised
red between my hipbones.
After my son was born they rebuilt
me with metal staples.

I don't know beauty or love that burns
you to filaments or sadness that eats
its own tail, thick with salt. No vistas open,
no berries ripen in a dirty hand. I have
my small son's marigold earwax. I have
someone else's sleep.

Postpartum

A dead lizard floats in the pool while
a man climbs a palm tree, chainsaw
dangling from his waist.

A crane rises from a tidal bed,
thick with the brown muck
of coastal waters.

Dead crabs offer up
white porcelain legs,
splayed open like a hand.

I read the landscape
because my daughter cannot yet
speak and my foreign body

offers no augury.

Elizabeth Wants

*But the angel said to him, "Do not be afraid, Zechari'ah,
for your prayer is heard, and your wife Elizabeth will bear
you a son, and you shall call his name John." Luke 1:13*

My son is a son of dryness.
I could have told you
he would eat locusts.

We filled his hands with doves
and wild honey, because older
brothers are made of thorns.

How long does the miracle hold,
if I want another,
a daughter to stay close to home?

A daughter with no
angels, sideways in my arms,
collapsing into sleep?

So when I press my face
to hers, my mouth
to the bridge of her nose,

we fit. And when God comes
to claim his own, I am not
left with only a husband

who never spoke again, hating
the prayer that did not need
his body for an answer.

The Fisherman's Wife

Once upon a time there were a fisherman and his wife
who lived together in a filthy shack near the sea

—*The Brothers Grimm*

Now it is a koi pond,
and I watch the bodies slip

past— shifting against
shadows and rocks, black

smeared like soot across orange
or yellow. Only the eyes

and mouths are white and open.
Mouths cut holes into the surface

of water, whiskers stream against
scales deeper than egg yolk.

In my hands, flesh bristles, gills
pump and gasp, and the mouth

cuts tight circles in the air, cuts
circles in the flesh of my palm.

Each blazing hoop is larger than
the last. Each bright ring expands
until I am swallowed by gold.

For Jen, the Day After Your Stroke

Every five minutes you reel
from sleep. The stranded lucidity
of your eyes flashes, you touch
my hand, the stuffed animal, grasp
the photos I brought, my hand again.
One leg pumps, restless. Its twin,
silenced. Half your face knows me.

Dusk, St Simon's Island

The rabbits spend their days
submerged in shallows,
just ears and eyes breaking
the surface of dark
water ringed in sea-grass.

Sometimes, when I'm wading,
fur brushes my legs, a soft echo
of my mother's white coat.

Come evening, you can measure
distance in the round, quiet bodies
of marsh rabbits come ashore:
brown nails studding the green grass,
fastening the ground to the road,

the road itself anchored to August
by a moon doused in brine.

Flathead Lake

For Jon and Charlotte

The long hand of evening
will set horses just out of sight,
smudged dark against
barn doors and fences.

Ranunculus petals, orange
as young fire, will braid
through her hair like a crown
of tongues.

You will stand barefoot
in the grass of your childhood,
and she will place her hands
on your face and answer you

because tonight is your wedding.
Her hands will curve
like the shoreline of the lake,
cold and patient. Still.

A Love Poem for Ellen, Ten Years Late

I remember your short hair,
sports bra, open flat hips,
how every class,
I wanted to touch you—

a body is not what is desired
but the desire itself. So.

Put the tongue back
into my mouth and let me
say, the body never answers,
the body only asks.

November

Light walks out of the trees, past empty fields
that once housed apples, and warns
that soon snow will fall in the orange, metallic
evenings.

Light closes the doors to the barns
and asks us where will we hide when the elms
collapse and as we pause to answer,

light empties our pockets and fills our windows
with nothing but the cries of our dogs hunting
in their sleep and the pulse of our blood,
thrumming with heat.

Plate Tectonics

An eighth grade earth science
field trip brought us to the planetarium.

The speaker lectured about the travel
of continents, where they shake.

He built every fact on comets:
we have been banged into shape

by shooting stars, he claimed,
with no mention of plate tectonics.

Did he know he had slipped
to the other side of fact,

that fault lines, not comet
smacks, run to our centers?

Or does it happen too quickly, same
podium, same small state museums?

I knew he was wrong.

The Last Dog

Home I think   home and I smell now and the green
sweep of here and the lemon sharp of

tomatoes growing over and over themselves   home
then and now and under me the fat

beards of irises the open throats of daffodils under dirt and
home of roses cornflowers

bright blurs against the switch and lift of a squirrel's tail I can
taste metal and fur but it's gone

and I want   home and sleep and I count my bones
as I settle and rise

          home in my hips   home strung out across the
beams of my body my   home I

am pressed to your legs spilling across your bed warm breath on
your neck, were you gone

you are home   were you gone now I am as close as heat
as close as hunger because I

bring my hunger to you and you say yes which is love which is
hunger and always your hands

the constant surprise of what I already love.

Carrion Birds

By the road, hunched like old women,
a cluster of birds, heavy shouldered
and menacing. Surely the dark
shine of their bodies means buzzards,
means death or something similar,
sliced into the red of cranberry bog
and I think about drowning, or floating
like those sharp-tasting berries,
drifting up and free for the harvest.
I think a flood like that would be better
than this drive to my mother's house.
I want the water to rise slowly, to rise
kindly, the way they say you can boil
lobsters by gently turning up the heat.
They won't even notice. I wish
the heavy bodied birds are osprey,
taloned fish hawks drifted inland,
ready to swoop, not buzzards waiting
to find what has already died.
They will be here tomorrow:
the bog, the birds, the low
stone walls of an old town.
Carrion birds and the long
drive to my mother's house.

Portrait in Wikipedia Entry for Fentanyl

mimic

dissolving
through the skin

troublesome
imprecision
dissolves

cheeks   tongue gums

indefinitely postponed

The precise reason

folded
confusion

hundreds of times more potent

uncovered

degradation

Traces

small

less

At Twenty-Six Weeks, A Fetus Starts Dreaming

The last time my mother
stayed here, I heard her
scream in her sleep,
banishing demons
    in the name of the Lord Jesus Christ.

What an inheritance.

Could you hear her, tucked
away, still safely within
me, as she commanded
those evil spirits to depart?

Are you a charismatic
pastor in your dreams,
speaking in tongues, raising
your arms in exhortation?

Can I hope for some
kinder influence, the way
I see your father
in your long fingers?

He sleeps like he eats,
untroubled, as simple
as closing his eyes until
he opens them again.

Or will you, like your mother,
fall asleep last and wake
first, quick to hear
the dream stutters of others—

not a sleeper but a witness to sleep.

Parking Lot

My mother says *the burden*
of you in my life
is worse than the death of my
first daughter.
I am sitting in my car
outside the school where I teach,
in a parking lot.
Pine needles fall on my windshield
and I say: *that isn't appropriate,*
when I want to say: Mom. Please.
I have a daughter now.
So I stay on the phone, waiting
for one of us to be a mother
as she repeats, *having you in my life.*
You are worse. My first daughter.
The next time she calls,
I will remind her of this and she will say,
Oh. I thought I said that to your brother.
Anyway. It's true.

To Stone

Each night ends in sugar.
My daughter grasps
for plums fast as I peel them.

She eats one, reaches
for the next, smiling,
slapping the table,

and then settles into the new
work of sweetness.
I eat the plum

skins piling up, taste the dark
purple in my mouth, her smacks
of pleasure. Daughter,

it won't last; my own mother
called today, named
the ways I've failed her.

Some nights, you wake
and I am the wrong answer.

This is all I want:
your need and my reply,
plums eaten to stone.

Elizabeth Asks

Now after those days his wife Elizabeth conceived; and she hid herself five months. Luke 1:24

The holy question of how much will it hurt.

Mary, come and braid my hair,
the men inside us have spoken
and we know they will speak again.

But for now I am adrift in my own body.
Mary, where are the limits of promise?

No one offers a miracle a crib.
No one says, Elizabeth, do you need blankets?
Can your old fingers knit what is needed?

Will milk come? Will the weight of my limbs
rise from my body like mist burned by daylight?

Practice with me, Mary.
Let me rub your temples and sing softly.
None of us knows how to mother.

Acknowledgments

All We Can Hold: A Collection of Poetry on Motherhood: "Egret"

cahoodaloodaling: "Elizabeth Wants"

Gravel: "Break My Hands"

Heartwood Literary Magazine: "Ownership"

Psaltery and Lyre: "A Body Made of Bees"

Menacing Hedge: "When I Became a Mother," "Annunciation,"
     "Red Right Returning," "The Fisherman's Wife"

Milk Teeth Anthology: Hermeneutic Chaos: "Minnow," "To Stone"

Rappahannock Review: "Honeysuckle"

Rogue Agent: "Moths," "Clean"

Ruminate Magazine: "Mary Remembers," "Elizabeth Asks"
     (winner of the 2017 Elizabeth B McCabe Prize)

San Pedro River Review: "November"

The Fem: "Postpartum"

The Hopper: "Reservoir," "Dusk"

This Body I Live In: Slim Volume III: "Bless"

Tinderbox Poetry Journal: "Carolina Wrens"

Whale Road Review: "Fiddler Crab"

Wild Horses: The Women on Fire Series (ELJ): "Driving Past Midnight in Rural Tennessee," "Buzzards Bay," "Larches," "Oophorectomy," "The Body, After"

The following poems previously appeared in the chapbook, *Bury the Lede,* published by Finishing Line Press: "Town Waits Politely for Dead Whale to Explode," "Bridges Freeze Before Roads," "Before the First Snow"

I have so many thank yous. Here are some:

Thank you to my children—I love you both with my whole heart. Thank you to my husband. You make all poems possible.

Thank you to my parents, Frank and Anne, who taught me to love words. To my brother, Frank, who is a poet as well. To Jennifer, John, Jean, Liz, Eric, and Lauren. Thank you for your love and support.

Thank you, Rick Barot for changing my life with your incredible teaching. Thank you to April Alvarez and John Grammer for making Sewanee a true home.

Thank you to my thesis advisor, Andrew Huggins, whose comments brought my work to life.

Thank you to my dearest writer friends. Team Sleigh: Erin and Tomas. The Downtown House girls: Hanna, Mary, and Kathryn. The Rivendell poets: Carly, Dwight, and Darby. To my whole summer family at The Sewanee School of Letters. My Atlanta poets: Kathleen, Trish, Karen, Jen DT, Sally, and everyone who has made me welcome. And the incredible teachers of The Westminster Schools in Atlanta, GA.

Thank you to Josh Ralston, Bianca and Lydia Dorman, and Daniel Inman for showing me a faith that welcomes wrestling.

Thank you to the friends who celebrated me: Gremlin, Siena, Freshman Jon, Maureen, Tati, Missy, Vicki, Jess AB, James Arthur, and Ryan Sample. If no one else reads this book, your kind words are more than enough reward.

Thank you to Jane Simpson who believed these poems could be a book.

Thank you to Molly Sutton Kiefer who made these poems an actual book. And Nikkita who made it beautiful.

To all the friends, colleagues, family, teachers, professors, and other writers who have lifted me and loved me along the way, thank you, as my daughter would say: FOREVER. AND TWICE.

And finally, thank you to that one very nice nun who chatted with me on a sunny summer day at Stirling's Coffeehouse's lawn. When I mentioned I was writing something called VISITATION, you responded with a pithy remark about a young virgin and an old woman who believed herself barren. *Could you imagine what they talked about?*

You asked me that question, and in that moment, gave me a book. Thank you.

A graduate of The Sewanee School of Letters MFA program, Maggie Blake Bailey has poems published or forthcoming in *Foundry, Ruminate, Rust & Moth,* and elsewhere. Her chapbook, *Bury the Lede,* is available from Finishing Line Press. She teaches in Atlanta, GA, where she lives with her husband and two young children. *Visitation* is her debut collection.